Postcards from the Underworld

THE ARAB LIST

Postcards from the Underworld
Poems

SINAN ANTOON

Translated from the Arabic by the Poet

Seagull
BOOKS

LONDON NEW YORK CALCUTTA

Seagull Books, 2023

Arabic originals and English translations © Sinan Antoon, 2023

This English compilation © Seagull Books, 2023
First published by Seagull Books, 2023

ISBN 978 1 80309 250 8

British Library Cataloguing-in-Publication Data
A catalogue record for this book is available from the British Library

Typeset by Seagull Books, Calcutta, India
Printed and bound by Wordsworth India, New Delhi, India

CONTENTS

Prayer

our Iraq, which art in dust
hallowed be thy name
thy hellfire come
thy will be done on earth
as it is in heaven
give us this day our daily death
and forgive us not our betrayals
as we forgive not those who betray us
and lead us not into temptation
for we are dead tired
amen

Psalm

In the beginning was the stab
The dagger made the wound
in its own image
then went away

searching
for another body

The wound wept
for forty days
then healed

It became a heart
and crawled away

searching
for another body

The Day

And then the day came
when the earth was spent
and overbled
and lost its gravity
the leaves stopped falling
dead birds too
their corpses kept flying
up into the grey sky
which had become
a colossal screen
of the underworld

The New God

We looked at the map
All those rivers we had crossed
searching for that new god
the priests said
he was born for our sake
When we reached his homeland
We found crowds
marching in his funeral procession
We joined them
They told us
of all those rivers they had crossed
searching for the new god
the priests said
he had died for their sake

From the Lost Gospels

He cried
ten thousand years
to fill the seas
then went away
without leaving an address
or sending any prophets
Nothing
but this rain
and wind

From Eve's Confessions

I was the voice of the wind
and when it grew tired
I descended from its ribs
and left it
weeping everywhere
for me

I walked on water
a thousand years
then created myself
on the earth's skin
and when I was bored
I made Adam
God was a mere game we played

Divine Failure

He always sat at the front row in that divinity school in a faraway galaxy. He listened devoutly and wrote down every word that came out of the teacher's mouth. He was a diligent god who learnt by heart all the secrets and tricks of creation, but he lacked talent.

And thus, after graduation, when he was given all that space, he took a shot at creating the Sun, just as he'd learnt in Genesis. But all he came up with instead were dead stars, which he dumped into the trash can of eternity. After thousands of dead stars, he finally managed to make the Sun. Then it was time for the Moon. That attempt produced piles of black holes and deformed discs that still roam through the outskirts of the universe, covering their faces in shame.

I Hear It

Perhaps it tripped and fell
off the musical scale
and is crawling
like a dying soldier

Perhaps it eluded
the player's fingers
so that it might fly away
towards a different song

Perhaps someone severed its tongue
mistaking it for a rose

Is it wailing
and bleeding in the dark

Have you seen it?
That stray note?
I never have
But I hear it so clearly

Blind Song

The same blind song
crosses my silence
at this time
every morning

Yesterday a bird carried it
The day before a butterfly
Today it clasps a cloud's hand
I don't know where it goes
or when it returns

Whenever I try to follow it
It pushes me away
Saying:
Not yet!

The Saz Player

His undulating voice
mimics the distant topography
on the slopes of that village

he left behind
His fingers argue with the strings
Rephrasing the same questions

Was his village flooded
by blood?
Or wiped off the map by a state?

His voice calls out
to a stray horse
which is the untameable agony
inhabiting every form

A bird that lost its nest
has been building a nest of thorns
for years now
in the singer's throat
where it sleeps alone

A bird now hungry as the deer
that survived the massacre
and hid in the singer's memory

The song is hungry
looking for a morsel of bread
But this whole scene
means very little to tourists

Garment

With words
and the eye's needle
I sew this garment
for silence

I thread a stray cloud
to a feather from an extinct bird
the dust of a star
to a fallen leaf

When I finish
The angel of nihilism
standing before me
slips it on
but unsatisfied
casts it off again
and yawns

I take up another thread

A Heavy Heart

I've finally understood
that the heart is a box
I can empty its sorrow
and fill it up with joy
whenever I wish
I don't always succeed
At times it becomes too heavy to carry
so I put it aside and lean on it
Then I get up and carry it again

To be fair, there are times
when it's quite light
It spreads its wings and soars
reminding me
that I am its nest

. . .

But these are the requisite illusions
for a poem

The truth is this:
The heart is a long shelf
stacked with heavy boxes
No wings
Just dust and pain

I lied, again (for the poem's sake of course)

But, since we are approaching
the last few lines,
I will come clean:

I know nothing about your hearts
I only know that mine is an old palace
So vast I used to wander and get lost in it

Today its rooms and corners
are stacked with hundreds of boxes.

There is not much space left
Except for this narrow spot by the gate
where I squat
and write
this poem

Visitation

I visit my grave
quite often
It's nearby
No one knows its location
except me

I never pray there
I might shed a tear
or two
for no specific reason

But on happy days
I pluck a flower
place it on the tombstone
in my lapel

. . .

and smile

In My Next Life

In my next life
I will not be I

I will be a wild flower
Lying on the slope of a distant hill
butterflies will alight on it
A child who never lived through war
will pluck it
and take it to his mother
will place it between her breasts
She will kiss him
and smell me
and I will smell her

. . .

In my next life
I will not be

A Feather

For Ibtisam

Did it fall off
A migrant bird's wing?

Or is it all that remains
Of a hungry fox's feast?

Is it a letter
From a language I cannot decipher?

'What is your name?'
I ask
Do you yearn
For that wing?

It doesn't answer

I will carry it
Call it *You*
and make it
the poem's tentpole

Autumn in Heaven

Trees are evergreen
gentle winds
tickle their branches
The elders read newspapers
Children play
their mothers watch
There are rumours
that another angel
committed suicide
last night

Train of the Dead

No need for tickets
the angel smiles:

'It will be a short trip'
Then points to an empty compartment
Its bed made of mist
Its pillows of clouds

Loved ones stand outside waving

. . .

The train is on its way
But I hear nothing

In the compartment next to mine
A man holds his severed head
And cries

Interval

The Bellagio Cemetery gate was open
I went in
a guest of the dead
I'm a stranger here
I know no one
my family's tombs
far away in a distant homeland

Silence
flowers wilting on marble
and stone
grass keeping company
to the unvisited

Each name on the tombstone
followed by two dates

Two arms

one takes us out of the womb
The other places us in the tomb

With a brief dash
in between:

—

. . .

I left the cemetery
and went on walking
on my own dash

Bellagio, July 2018

Murmur

Just before dying
the man who inhabited me
for many years
murmured:
I want to stay here
with you

I carry his remains
and every morning
we put on a new shroud

Black Butterfly

This black butterfly
is a minute
that fled a dead night
It is looking for a rose
to place on the night's tomb
But it has no fingers
and the roses are heavy

Birth Certificate

Is it a wounded bird? This thing that lies dying in the lap of a woman whose corpse is propped against the trunk of a giant mulberry? When its tiny wings flutter they splash her face with blood. Flies circle her gaping mouth. Her eyes are staring at hell. It wails like a human.

No, it isn't a bird. It's a cherub covered in blood. It was startled and tried to hide when it saw me. I saw a knife covered with dirt and blood. I picked it up. I held the cherub by its wings. It shivered like the branches of the tree. I severed its umbilical cord. A cry soared. I decided to rid it of its wings. I whispered:

'The heavens are no more safe than the earth.'

When I placed it on the ground, it crawled away in search of its first prey.

Another Day

The day starts its day
with hope
Looking into the mirror
it dreams of being different
Not just another day
But a day of monumental events
that will change the world
and rouse humans from their slumber

It makes its way around the earth

. . .

And then we see it in its last hours
as it returns
exhausted
like a shabby homeless man
blinded by blood

It returns,
having discovered
it's just another day

Rest Your Horns

The wind is a raging bull tonight
saddled with stabs
and bolting everywhere
The sky howls
All the doors are shut
Everyone is asleep
except me

I stand
and wait for it

I wave my heart
like a cap
and say:
Rest your horns
right here
Let us bleed
together

The Poet

The poet is another Noah
He spends a lifetime
building an ark of words
filling it with metaphors and clouds
his solitude a mast
But he makes sure
there is enough silence
in the skeleton
so that the waters might seep into his poem
and it sinks
until it rests
at the bottom of the sea

Slow Mail

I am all alone here
wandering
a barren galaxy
No meteors and no . . .
By the time my light
reaches your eyes
I will have been
extinguished
and your eyes
will be
ashes
wandering
in the wind

Days Like This

... of the desire
often felt
on days like this
to abandon this shape
of being
and become a cloud
or tree
or poem

to liquefy the *I*
evaporate
into a cloud
roaming
but eventually performing
its end
by kissing
the million lips
of a tree
the last tree
of what once was
a forest

someone is there
gazing at the tree
thinking
of the desire. . .

Dismemberment

The body, or a voice impersonating it, said:
Go! As of now, you are all free.
The eyes flew far away, joining flocks of other eyes.
which had filled the sky, almost blocking the sunlight.
The lips parted company without a farewell;
One searched for a new face,
the other for a lip that would listen to its complaints.
The tired tongue sought a mute man's mouth to rest in.
The hands clapped and waved to each other as they fled.
The right leg appeared frightened and hesitant,
then rushed to catch up with the left.
The nose fell on the ground. . .
As for the heart, it kept beating alone
until a stray foot crushed it.

A Head

I was no tree
or sheep

but they muttered a few words
and chopped my head off
with a dull knife
It rolled away and I saw myself
kneeling
hands tied behind my back
The fountain of blood died down
a few seconds later
and they went away
never looking back
Hours later came the hungry dogs
sniffing at me

'Take your share
leave nothing
of my body'
But, I begged them,
'Please,
leave my head
right here
at the bottom
of this poem'

Afterwords

My father's warm palms shielded my ears. I could hear his blood racing in his veins. As if being chased by the bombs falling outside. My mother's lips fluttered like a terrified butterfly. She was talking to God and asking him to protect us. That's what she did during the last war. And He'd listened. Her arms were clasped around my two sisters. Maybe God could not hear her this time. The bombing was so loud. After our house in Jabalya was destroyed, we hid in the UNRWA school. But the bombs followed us there too . . .

and found us.

*

Mother and father lied
We didn't stay together
I walked alone for hours

They lied
There are no angels
Just people walking
Many of them children

The teacher lied too
My wounds didn't become anemones
like that poem we learnt in school

*

Sidu didn't lie
He was there
Just as he'd promised me
before he died
He is here
I found him
Leaning on his cane
Thinking of Jaffa
When he saw me
He spread his arms wide
Like an eagle
A tired eagle with a cane
We hugged
He kissed my eyes

*

–Are we going back to Jaffa, *sidu*?
–We can't
–Why?
–We are dead
–So are we in heaven, *sidu*?
–We are in Palestine, *habibi*
and Palestine is heaven
. . .
and hell
–What will we do now?
–We will wait
–Wait for what?
–For the others
. . .
to return

An Ordinary Day

It was an ordinary day
except for father being very late
mother screamed when she opened the door
He was headless
and his clothes were smeared with blood
He hugged her to calm her down, but she kept crying
He said he would no longer be able to watch TV with us
and that we would never eat together again
He gave his pillow to my little brother
told us to listen to mother
and do our homework
Then he knelt in prayer
thanking God for what was left
My little sister cried a lot
then beheaded her doll
and buried its head
in our back yard

Letter to al-Mutanabbi

You were right
Your words are still wings of light
always carrying you to us
sometimes carrying us to you

Your name is a green tattoo
on Baghdad's tired face
Your street the forehead
of a body beheaded every morning

Just another chapter
in the saga of blood and ink
you knew so well

I cannot lie to you
I'm quite pessimistic
we are still etching
the walls of this cave
thousands of years long

with signs we keep reinterpreting
and myths about a future world
where we don't devour one another
where the sun is friendly
and the seas cannot inherit our fever

Some are digging
a deeper grave
about to embrace us all
they, too, have their engravings,
maps, philosophers and books

We can only keep dreaming
of a shore for the wind
and dig wells
in the dark
with fingernails of silence and solitude
we will weave an ocean out of ink
for our myths
and out of words a sail
or a shroud
vast enough for all.

Every book is a well
around which we sit
drinking to your health
trying to live
as you did
with death and after it

Al-Mutanabbi (10th century) was one of the greatest Arab poets.
Al-Mutanabbi Street, in the heart of old Baghdad, is the cultural
centre of the city with tens of bookshops and stalls, and the famous
Shahbandar café where the literati congregated every Friday. On
5 March 2007, a bomb exploded on that street, killing 26 civilians
and destroying many of the bookshops.

A Photograph

Of an Iraqi Boy on the Front Page of the New York
Times

He sat
at the edge of the truck
(eight or nine years old?)
surrounded by his family
His father
mother
and five siblings
all asleep
His head was buried
in his hands
All the clouds of the world
were waiting
at the threshold of his eyes
The tall man wiped off the sweat
from his brow
and started digging
the seventh grave

One Night; In Many Cities

We leant on the trunk
of a palm tree
which has been burning for years
Yet its shadow insists
on keeping us company
even on cold nights
Fronds wave farewell
through the windows of an old song
about the river
before its waves choke on
the corpses
The song drowns in the river
we sit on a third bank
everywhere
watching
There is enough wine tonight
for the ghosts of the dead
who have just joined our table
. . .

Tomorrow
we must strip their corpses
from the song

and shroud them
with words

Heard on New Year's Eve

One war to another:
May you never tire!
May we go on
forever

One book to its neighbour:
Hoping someone will remember us
That his fingers touch our leaves
and rouse us from this dust
if for only a minute

I hope we stay together
and if a saw were to break our backs
may our remains stay close by
Perhaps two chairs
around an elegant table?

One cloud to another:
Are you tired of travelling?
No worries, soon we'll sleep
in the sea

A sea to itself:
I am bored with these shores
and with everyone on them
I wish I could become a cloud
and fly far away

A Handbag in China Town

Green
dangling like a tropical fruit
its shiny skin calling out

A hand reaching out
feels it

thinking to pluck it
The branch bowing its head
. . .
It is so far now
from the fingers that stitched it
fingers that now dangle
like dry branches
from a tiny body
asleep on a mattress
whose threads groan
from exhaustion
on the other side
of this world

New York, July 2008

A Butterfly in New York

I chased it so often
in our Baghdad garden
but it would always fly away
today
three decades later
in another continent
it alights on my shoulder
As blue as the sea's thoughts
or a dying angel's tears
its wings two leaves
falling from heaven
But why now?
Does it know
that I no longer chase
butterflies
only watch them in silence?
And that I live
as a broken branch?

Winesong

For Malihe and Shahram

The tears of a cloud
after losing her sisters
The sun's blush
as it gazes upon its own nudity
The wind's whispers
to the vines
Its secrets
as it rests its head
on the earth's shoulder
The wavering of a red butterfly
amid lavender
The sighs of a goddess
whose worshippers are extinct
The desire awaiting
in a widowed body

The sorrow of a shore
at the ebbing of the sea
The joy of silk
when it touches a breast
Two nipples vying
for a mouth

The howling of a blind wolf
on a moonless night
The gasps of earth
and
the seeds
of a thousand poems
are
in this drop
of red wine

I Don't Visit My Mother

I don't visit my mother
that often
Her house is at the end of the world
always cold
even in the Baghdad summer
The last time I visited her
she said little
Silence was a stone
still weighing heavily on me
Even her neighbours were silent
They stared at me
eyes shut
The wind murmured
something
I couldn't understand
Then the guard at the cemetery
extended his hand
and said:
'May she rest in peace'

Angels on My Ceiling

'This city has demons'
a German friend told me
Yes, but it has angels, too
I see them every morning
in my apartment
staring from the ceiling
I counted twenty-five or so
with tiny wings and tired faces
as if about to say something
But they just silently stare

What do they want?
Sometimes I forget that they are there
and go about my life
until the day one of them breaks its wings
and falls next to my bed
its head scattered all over the floor
tired of its heavy burdens
It's not easy being an angel these days
I don't touch it
The Lord appears the next morning
looks at it with no pity whatsoever
sweeps its remains with a broom
throws the wing into the trash

and says, in a heavy German accent:
It's an old building, you know?
I'll get someone to fix the cracks
in the other ones
Hopefully, no more fallen angels, Ja?

Berlin, June, 2009

Angelus Novus

I reside as much with the dead as with the unborn.

—Paul Klee

The storm is napping
under the angel's wings
but your new angel
still looks back
at us
The storm will soon awaken
and continue its work
War is beautiful
here
in your painting
on a wall in Berlin
your colours have tamed it so well
The paper has absorbed so much of the cry
I have one question for you:
What shall I do
when I exit the museum?
As soon as I am out on the street
I have to face the piles of corpses
Benjamin saw in your painting
Historians and journalists have yet to reach a consensus
regarding the body count

I'm not sure either
Progress has yet to cease
and my pillow is crowded
with ghosts

An Alternative History

'What if there were an alternative history? Do you want to see what could have happened had we let reason guide us?' He sounded serious and then pointed to a screen with icons for centuries and years. 'Everything is here.'

I tapped 'Twentieth Century' and then 'World War II' and 'Germany'.

The first scene (black and white): Adolf Hitler, an arts teacher in a small school in Berlin. Married to Eva Braun, a secretary with an average salary. They have one child, Hans, who looks like his father. The family lives a relatively simple life. Eva dreams of a bigger apartment and of visiting Paris or Rome when the war is over. Adolf is moody and has a temper, but he is a good father—a peaceful, contented man, and a proud German.

The second scene (black and white): Eva and Adolf standing amid crowds that line the street to greet the Führer's convoy. They all cheer and applaud the Führer who raises his right arm like a spear.

'I want to see the Führer, Daddy,' says Hans. Adolf lifts him up on his shoulder. Hans is elated as he waves to the Führer and shouts with the others, 'Sieg Heil . . . '

Adolf feels pride, but a bit of jealousy too. But he never communicates his inner thoughts. Not even to Eva. She might think he's mad.

Berlin, April 2009

49

Crossing

Here
at the El Paso airport
I wait for Valentina
who will take me to the other side
to read poems like this one
in Juarez
Valentina is late
soldiers standing in line
laughing
teasing one another
I was going to write: like hyenas
on the scent of their prey
But I shouldn't dehumanize them,
right?
They are peaceful now
waiting
their uniforms the colour of desert sand
their boots clean
ready
to step on the sands
of faraway faces
There
where other men and women
form long lines
to await their death

Phosphorus

When I was a kid
the tail end of my bike
had a red reflector

It glowed in the dark
just like the eyes of a cat
illuminated by the headlights
of distant cars

Tiny bits of phosphorus

Tiny bits of phosphorus
white phosphorus
illuminated the skies of Falluja
years ago
Now
infants there are born
with two heads
or
without eyes

Crazy Horse

Crazy Horse was not a crazy horse. He was an Apache child who ran faster than the wind so his mother called him 'Crazy Horse'. He rushed the seasons to grow up and defend the Apache. At night, he dreamt of one thing: to be a strong bird, to soar in the belly of the sky, to nest in the clouds, to pounce on the white man who hunted his ancestors like deer and scattered them in Arizona. But fever chased his soul from his body. It settled in a passing cloud. His body slept in a ditch. He never became that fierce bird.

It was three years before the Apache's final defeat. When five thousand soldiers besieged Geronimo and dragged him and his men in shackles (Skeleton Canyon, Arizona, 4 September 1886). All that is left of the Apache today are reservations on the margins of history.

. . .

An embedded reporter on the evening news in 2004 was about to be taken on a tour with US soldiers in a Humvee outside Baghdad. As they left the gate of al-Taji camp, the soldier-guide tells the reporter (and us): 'This is Indian country.' Brian Williams quoted a general using the same sentence as they flew over Iraq several years later. 'Crazy Horse' was the call sign for several Apache helicopters shown in footage released by *WikiLeaks* in 2010. They were firing missiles on Iraqi civilians, including children, and killing them, in Baghdad on 12 July 2007.

Do dreams die with their dreamers? Or do they roam the night searching for someone to dream them all over again? Perhaps they become nightmares dwelling in the sleep of others.

Apaches hover now in distant skies. And the hunt goes on.

Anamorphosis / Iraq

I.

19 November 2005

> Haditha, Al-Anbar Province, Iraq
> Kilo Company, Third Battalion, First Marine
> Division
>
> . . .
>
> Twenty-four unarmed Iraqi civilians
> Including:
> A seventy-six-year-old amputee
> In a wheelchair
> Holding a Qur'an
> A mother and child bent over
> Six children ranging in age from one to fourteen
>
> . . .
>
> Execution style

II.

December 2005

> The US military paid $2,500 (condolence payments)
> per victim to families of fifteen of the dead Iraqis. A
> total of $38,000.

III.

'Shoot first, ask questions later' were Sgt Wuterich's orders to his men as they searched nearby homes after a roadside bomb attack killed one Marine and injured two others.

IV.

21 December 2006

Eight marines are charged.

V.

17 June 2008

Six had their cases dropped and a seventh was found not guilty.

VI.

23 January 2012

Staff Sgt Frank Wuterich, 31, of Meridien, Connecticut, pleaded guilty to negligent dereliction of duty as the leader of the squad. The manslaughter charges were dropped.

VII.

24 January 2012

Wuterich was sentenced to a reduction in rank. He received a general discharge under honourable conditions. No jail time.

VIII.

Asked if he would have done anything differently that day, Salinas, one of the witnesses, said: 'I would have utilized my air to just level the house.'

Another witness, Dela Cruz, admitted that he urinated on the skull of one of the Iraqis he and Wuterich had shot.

IX.

19 August 2012

Meridien, Connecticut

Wuterich, who lives in California, returned home to Meridien, Connecticut, for a golf tournament organized by local veterans for his benefit.

'The tournament was organized by veterans' groups, including the Polish Legion of American Veterans, the American Legion and Marine Corps League Silver City Detachment.'

Bill Zelinsky, commander of the Polish Legion Sons Detachment, said combat veterans he's spoken with don't find fault with Wuterich's actions in Haditha.

'Any of the veterans in this club that I spoke to said
they would have handled the situation the same way
Frank did,' Zelinsky said. 'I have to believe he did the
right thing.'

X.

Haditha, Al-Anbar Province, Iraq

The twenty-four corpses are at home
in The Martyrs' Graveyard
Graffiti
on a wall in one of the deserted homes
of one of the families reads:
'Democracy assassinated the family that lived here.'

We Shall Wait

My face is an old painting
hanging on the wall
of a locked room
in an abandoned house

My only neighbour is this spider
which begins its day
whispering:

'Still here?
I shall weave us an exquisite web
and we shall wait.'

Letter to My Ancestor

Dear Ancestor,

I hope all is well. I am not sure if this letter will find its way to you, because I have no knowledge as to the whereabouts of your bones, that is, if anything is left. Nevertheless, I have been conversing with you for years now and arguing in my own language, which surely differs from the system you used to communicate. But nowadays they say that it is necessary to confront enemies and loved ones alike and to find 'closure'.

I have been thinking a great deal about the consequences of what you did and how everything changed afterwards. Therefore, I decided to write this letter to you. I want to unburden myself. I have so many questions and queries, but I must start with a bone I have been meaning to pick with you. Every now and then, they publish something here or there about a new discovery or theory explaining the monumental decision you and your comrades took centuries ago. And the question haunts me: What came over you? Why did you step down from the throne? Why, for God's sake, did you abandon the trees and their branches? Those steeped in knowledge say that it was the search for sustenance or some grass to chew on. So it was competition and survival that forced you to walk on your two feet (our backs still ache from it, by the way) and not wanderlust, as some imagine. Your descendants kept on running and running for thousands of years until they reached these caves in whose darkness we are still warring. We have inscribed a great deal on the walls of these caves, Grandpa. Since then, we have been falling into this abyss. I just wish you had held on tightly to that branch! You would have saved us from all this and I would not have had to write this to you.

Regretfully,
Sinan Antoon

The Angel's Trumpet

We have made your sleep deep
The day the trumpet is blown and you come in droves
—Qur'an

The wind's hand dances
with the angel's trumpet
It doesn't blow it
This trumpet is neither of copper
nor bones
. . .
I am not Israfel
Even if I were
I wouldn't blow the angel's trumpet
I would let it wither away
and let the dead slumber on
forever

The Day's Catch

The day shuts its last eyes
My arms are tired oars
I drag my nets back to my bed
and empty out the minutes
dead fish

This Was Not Written

We toil in silence day and night. Our hands are lacerated from rowing and our backs are hunched from all the corpses we carry. Our feet are chained to the bottom of the boat where we sleep. Crows hover above and swoop down to steal the crumbs. We aren't allowed to speak. The only sound we hear is cawing and the slap of oars hitting the water.

A week ago, after I dragged the last corpse in the batch, I forgot the rules and muttered to myself 'When will we be saved? When will this flood be over? This was not written in the books.' One of the guards, standing on the shore like a spear, heard me. He laughed out loud and whipped me, shouting:

'Books? You idiot! Even Noah has been working for us for ten thousand years. The flood will go on forever.'

Then he kicked the boat with his foot and spat on me. 'Come back with more corpses and don't waste time with these silly thoughts. Or I will chop off your head and give it as a toy to my son.'

A Postcard from the Underworld

I have never seen the Sun
It does not rise here
My father saw it, there, before his death
He tells me about it all the time,
about its ever-burning flames.
'Like a candle,' he said,
lit by the gods
Never to be extinguished,
like the one I am holding now.
Here
he taught me
how to put these bodies back together
to cover them with feathers
so they could roam the darkness.
Sometimes an arm or a leg remains
I put it in the corner
and wait for the piles they bring
the next day
I will ask my father about the eye
he hung on the wall a week ago
It is still shedding tears
I wonder if it is longing for its sister
or for the Sun?

Nostalgia for Light

Place your right
or left ear
to the ground
and listen!

Do you hear moons
choking on dirt?

Trees gasp
extend their roots
to kiss the foreheads
of the newly dead
Branches shiver
and the wind has nothing
to say now

Night is in mourning

But other lips
will rise tomorrow
to repeat
the same words
and kiss the sun

A New Sun

Every sleeping tear
shall wake up
and look for her sisters
to form a river

Every voice
shall rise from its grave
looking for a throat
to build a nest
for a chant

Every word
dreams
of standing in that phrase
we use to plough the sky
and plant a new sun:

'The people want. . .'

Psalm

Martyrs do not go to paradise
Its gates have been shut for centuries
The merchants who buy its rivers
look down from their lofty balconies
at the long lines
of the homeless
hovering outside

Martyrs do not go to paradise
They leaf through the heavenly book
each in their own way
as a bird
a star
a cloud.

They appear to us every day
and cry for us
We, who still linger
in this hell they tried to extinguish
with their blood

Scene

The sun is neutral
in performing its task
the sky is silent (clouds have fled)
the wind is fatigued

scattered trees
count corpses

Wars

When I was torn by war
I took a brush
and soaked it with death
and drew a window
on the wall of this war

I opened it
searching
for something

But all I saw
was another war

and a mother
weaving a shroud
for the dead man
still in her womb

A Prisoner's Song

For the POWs of the Iraq–Iran War 1980–88 . . .
on both sides

From the distant fog
after the communiqués had withered
and the canons had stopped spitting
he returned
covered with 'there'
His silence an umbrella
under our ululation
he passed by us
through us
to his old room
The lute still there
its strings in their wooden exile
yearned for his rainy fingers

But he never touched it
What language could explain
how eight years
had gnawed away
ten fingers

To an Iraqi Infant

Do you know
that your mother's nipples
are dry bones?
That her breasts
are bursting
with depleted uranium?

Do you know
that the window of her womb
overlooks
a confiscated land?

Do you know
that your tomorrow
has no tomorrow?
That your blood
is the ink
of new maps?

Do you know
that your mother is weaving
the slowness of her moments
into an elegy?
And that she is already
mourning you?

Don't be shy!
Your funeral is over
The tears are dry
Everyone's gone

Come forward!
It's only a short way
Don't be late
Your grave is already looking
at its watch!

Don't be afraid!
We'll arrange your bones
whichever way you want
and leave your skull
on top

like a flower

Come forward!
your many friends await
more and more
Every day
. . .
Your ghosts
will play together

Come on!

New York, December 2002

A Prism; Wet with Wars

This is the chapter of
devastation

This is our oasis
An angle where wars intersect
Tyrants accumulate around our eyes
But our shackles leave enough space for applause
Let us applaud

Another evening climbs
the city's candles
Tech hooves trample the night
A people is being slaughtered across short waves,
but the radio vomits raw statements
and urges us to
applaud

With the skeleton of a burning umbrella
we receive this rain
A god sleeps on our flag
but no prophets on the horizon
Maybe they will come if we
applaud
Let us applaud

We will baptize our infants with smoke
plough their tongues
with flagrant war songs
or UN resolutions
Teach them the bray of slogans
and leave them beside burning nipples
in an imminent wreckage
and applaud

Before we weave an autumn for tyrants
we must cross this galaxy of barbed wires
and keep on repeating

Happy New War!

Baghdad, March 1991

Delving

The sea is a lexicon
of blueness
assiduously read
by the sun
your body, too
is a lexicon

of my desires
whose first letter
will take a lifetime

Beirut, April 2003

Phantasmagoria I

Blue rain
addressing a silent orchestra
on a distant morning
the maestro cannot read
the foggy lines

Butterflies bloom
from your vocal cords
and migrate to my memory

Baghdad, 1989

Phantasmagoria II

your lips
are a pink butterfly
fluttering
from one word
to another
I chase after them
in gardens
of silence

Cairo, June 2003

Sifting

My eyes
are two sieves
sifting
through piles of others
for you

Cairo, August 2003

The Milky Way

Your nipple
is a rounded decade
of strawberries
My tongue
a tribe
of motherless fingers
climbing
the marble dome
of a pagan temple

Angels wail for asylum

I swim in a fountain
of undeciphered languages
but
come morning
your bra
strangles
my metaphors

1989

Wrinkles on the Wind's Forehead

1

the wind is a blind mother
stumbling
over the corpses
no shrouds
save the clouds
but the dogs
are far quicker

2

the moon is a graveyard
for light
the stars are women
wailing

3

the wind, tired
from carrying coffins,
leaned
against a palm tree

A satellite inquired:
Where to, now?
the silence

in the wind's cane murmured:
'Baghdad'
and the palm tree
burst into flame

4

the soldier's fingers scrape
and scrabble
like question marks
or sickles
searching the womb
of the wind
for weapons
nothing but smoke
and depleted uranium

5

how narrow this strait
which sleeps
between two wars
yet which I must cross

6

My heart is a stork
perched on a distant dome
in Baghdad
its nest made of bones
its sky
of death

7

This is not the first time
the myths have washed their face
with our blood
(t)here they are
looking into the mirror of the horizon
as they don our bones

8

war salivates
tyrants and historians pant
a wrinkle smiles
on the face of a child
who will play
during a pause
between wars

9

The Euphrates
is a long procession
Cities pat its shoulders
as palm trees weep

10

The child plays
in time's garden
but war calls upon her
from inside:
come on in!

11

The grave is a mirror
into which the child looks
and dreams:
when will I grow up
and be like my father

dead

12

the Tigris and Euphrates
are two strings
upon death's harp

and we are songs
or fingers strumming

13

For two and a half wars
I've been here
in this room
whose window is a grave
I'm afraid of opening

There is a mirror on the wall
When I stand before it
naked
my bones break into a laugh
and I hear death's fingers
tickling the door

14

I place my ear
on the belly of this moment
I hear wailing
I place it on another moment:
I hear the same!

Cairo, May–June 2003

Strings

1

the player's fingers ascend
the musical scales
and carry me
to the clouds
and then descend
followed by God
who weeps
and apologizes for everything

2

the strings of the lute
pull my soul
from the well of silence
fill my heart
with the blue of the sea
storm my branches
pluck me
and scatter me off
to an island far away
outside time
inside my heart

3

this umbilical cord
extends from my heart
to the banks of the Euphrates
I sever it every morning
but, at night,
nostalgia
stitches it back

4

a thread
that rains from the needle's eye
through a night
whose blackness
tires the candles
that count its minutes

a thread used by a mother
to mend a shirt
that still remembers the scent
of the prisoner
whose return
she's been waiting
for eleven autumns

a shirt
no one will ever wear

5

a shelf
in the heart's archives
where postponed deaths
are stacked
next to rumours
of happiness

6

the borderline
across the provinces
of nostalgia
between a country
that never was
and a country
that will never be—
whenever it is pulled away
by imagination
there
history
brings it back
here

7

the sobbing of a man
as he clings to the thread
that runs from his fingers
towards a white kite
that still soars
in the skies of his childhood
outside the cell
on the night
of his execution

8

a silk thread
sighing
as it thinks of eloping
from a black bra
. . .
it is fatigued
it does not want to stop
two breasts
from kissing

9

an invisible ray
seizes my heart
the scent of a woman
passing by me

twenty years from now
had she not died
in the last war

10

the last line
in a manuscript
whose burning
has been delayed
for eight centuries

11

the migration route
taken by a rare bird
in its last season
before extinction

12

the shadow of the last palm tree
in a burning orchard
as its fronds comb
the wind's hair
and it receives consolation
from the sun

13
perhaps
the string is merely
a string
consoling the trees
crucified in the body of the lute
or is it just yearning
for another string
crucified
in a distant lute

Cairo, April–June 2003

A Sign

He pours whiskey on time
making a home in sleep
One wall is enough
for his back
Yesterday's paper provides a ceiling
Life is postponed
for now
But the ghosts still roam his past
always on time

panting
Every moment an open grave
A window to be shut
He quarrels with the void
He is mad, the passersby think
He places an ear to the ground
More graves are dug
Ghosts will wave from newspapers
He runs away
Leaving a piece of cardboard on the ground
GULF WAR VETERAN

From the Diary of a Ghost

When I died and was on my way to the graveyard, I was told that my life as a ghost would be great and that it would compensate for the miserable life I had lived before death.

'You will sleep all day in a comfortable grave where you can toss and turn as you wish. You will avoid all traffic, and daily suffering. You will wake up at night and roam your city freely and no one will be able to stop you and ask for your identification card. You will cross the street whenever you wish. No car will ever hit you. You will violate every law and travel to any country without having to obtain a visa. You will never feel hungry or thirsty and never experience cold or hot. No one will ever kill you, because you will be dead. You will be able to, if you wish, take revenge against your enemies. Your mere appearance will terrify those who oppressed you, who stole your money and killed you and your children. You will find pleasure in torturing them and turning their nights into hell. You will enter their houses whenever you wish. You will terrify their children and they will wet their beds. You will be the master and you will see them all kneeling before you like dogs, or running to a psychiatrist without telling anyone lest they be accused of madness. No medications will save them from you. You will return to your grave right before dawn every day, ecstatic about your power and singing your favourite song and planning for your next night.'

I have been roaming the streets of my city for many years now. No one sees me or is afraid of me. Not even the children. As for those who killed me, their fortunes have multiplied and their bellies are bigger. I sometimes get lost in their huge mansions. I often find them celebrating around their gigantic tables during laughter-filled nights. They don't notice or care when I pass by or enter. I stand next to their beds as they sleep and scream into their ears, but all I hear is their snoring getting louder. Their dogs are the only ones who greet me, sometimes barking or wagging their tails when I leave disappointed in the early morning, embarrassed by my failure. The grave is far narrower than I had imagined. I have not slept for almost a year. My neighbour advised me to go to therapy. He, too, said he had suffered the first few years, but then come to terms with the fact that we were twice deceived. I am writing this as I wait for my appointment.

Just Another Evening (in black & you)

1

Your voice floats
on the evening's water
a sleepy narcissus
I am a shore
which thinks of drowning

2

Every touch
is a white envelope
hiding tens of white letters
penned by your nudity
to itself

3

Your shirt
an open envelope
Your breasts
two letters
always
about to arrive

4

Even the night's fingers
whisper
as they think
of undressing you

Absence

When you leave
the place withers

I gather the clouds
scattered by your lips
and hang them on the walls
of my memory
awaiting
another morning

Afterword

I spent the formative years of my life (1967–1991) in Iraq. Baghdad, my hometown, has a rich cultural history. The heart of pre-modern Arab/ic culture for centuries, it attracted poets and philosophers—and plundering invaders as well. In the second half of the twentieth century, when modern Iraq was a nascent and promising society, Baghdad became the centre of modern Arabic poetry when Iraqi poets staged an aesthetic revolt against traditional forms. Being an Iraqi poet means inheriting a very rich poetic tradition. The great Palestinian poet, Mahmoud Darwish, once wrote 'be an Iraqi, my friend, to be a poet.'

I survived two wars—The Iran–Iraq War (1980–88) and the First Gulf War (1991). After leaving Iraq in 1991, I watched from afar as the United States wage another war in 2003. It invaded and occupied my city and country, to dismantle and destroy what its genocidal sanctions (1990–2003) didn't. This is the history that informs much of my writing. I should mention that I resent how 'our' writings (those of us who are from the global south) are often subjected to reductive readings, and I have written and spoken against 'the forensic interest in Arabic literature'.

The destruction of humans, habitats and homes is the legacy of colonial modernity. The United States, where I live, work and write, continues to be a most violent predator and perpetrator of destruction. As a poet, I find myself standing before the ruins of history (Iraq is but one site). It was obligatory for pre-modern Arab poets (my aesthetic ancestors and masters) to begin their poems by standing before the real or imagined ruins and remains of a beloved's encampment to contemplate and confront time and history. I have come to appreciate this iconic topos in the last few decades. The forms in which Arabic poetry is written have changed radically, but that topos crystallizes and encapsulates our encounter, as a species, with time, nature and history. What to say and write as one stands before the ruins. The ruins of one's life, city and homeland.

Sources

All the poems have been translated from Sinan Antoon, *Lalylun wāḥidun fī kull al-mudun* (Beirut/Baghdad: Manshūrāt al-Jamal, 2010) and *Kamā fī al-samā'* (Beirut/Baghdad: Manshūrāt al-Jamal, 2019).

'Crazy Horse' and 'Anamorphosis' were published in *Public Culture,* May 2022.

'The New God', 'The Day's Catch' and 'Garment' were published in *The Los Angeles Review,* June 2021.

'Visitation', 'A Heavy Heart', 'Autumn in Heaven', 'In the Beginning' and 'The Day' were published in *Critical Times* 2(1) (April 2019).

'Heard on New Year's Eve' was published in *Upstreet* 11 (2014).

'A Postcard from the Underworld' was published in *The Massachusetts Review* (Spring 2012).

'Phosphorus' was published in *Washington Square Journal* (Winter/Spring 2011).

'Crossing' and 'A Sign' were published in *Ploughshares* (Spring 2009).

'A Photograph', 'Clouds' and 'A Letter' were published in *World Literature Today* 81(5) (September–October 2007).

'Wars' 'A Prisoner's Song', 'To An Iraqi Infant', ' A Prism', 'Delving', 'Phantasmagoria I', 'Phantasmagoria II', 'Sifting', 'Wrinkles; On the Wind's Forehead', 'Strings', ' A Sign', 'Just Another Evening' and 'Absence' were published in *The Baghdad Blues* (White River Junction, VT: Harbor Mountain Press, 2007).

'Afterwords' was published in Vijay Prashad (ed.), *Letters to Palestine* (London: Verso, 2015).